BEST SIDE DISHES EVER

BEST
SIDE
DISHES
EVER

FOOLPROOF RECIPES
FOR GREENS, POTATOES,
BEANS, RICE, AND MORE

MONICA SWEENEY

Page 8: © stocknroll/iStockphoto.com; 10, 11: © nicolesy/iStockphoto.com; 12, 118: © -Ivinst-/iStock-photo.com; 15, 20, 26, 27, 28, 35, 40, 43, 44, 47: 52, 76, 91, 92: © bhofack2/iStockphoto.com; 16: © zi3000/iStockphoto.com; 19, 108, 111: © cobraphoto/iStockphoto.com; 23: © loooby/iStockphoto.com; 25: © ehaurylik/iStockphoto.com; 31: © otokimus/iStockphoto.com; 32: © nata_vkusidey/iStockphoto.com; 36: © rudisill/iStockphoto.com; 39, 55, 62, 63, 64, 74, 86, 107, 121: © Lauri Patterson/iStockphoto.com; 48: © JacobVanHouten/iStockphoto.com; 51: © edoneil/iStockphoto.com; 56: © hlphoto/iStockphoto.com; 59: © Katsiaryna Belaya/iStockphoto.com; 60, 70: © rudisill/iStockphoto.com; 66: © Zoryanchik/iStockphoto.com; 68: © chengyuzheng/iStockphoto.com; 72: © VeselovaElena/iStockphoto.com; 78: © Teleginatania/iStockphoto.com; 81: © violletta/iStockphoto.com; 82: © valeriopardi/iStockphoto.com; 83: © HandmadePictures/iStockphoto.com; 84, 85: © robynmac/iStockphoto.com; 88: © StephanieFrey/iStockphoto.com; 95: © komargallery/iStockphoto.com; 96: © rbananka/iStockphoto.com; 99: © pawelwizja/iStockphoto.com; 100, 101, 112, 114: © Olha_Afanasieva/iStockphoto.com; 102: © msheldrake/iStockphoto.com; 104: © Sarsmis/iStockphoto.com; 116: © ALLEKO/iStockphoto.com; 122: © minadezhda/iStockphoto.com; 125: © VankaD/iStockphoto.com

Cover (clockwise from top right): © rudisill/iStockphoto.com; © 4kodiak/iStockphoto.com; © violleta/iStockphoto.com; © Anna Kurzaeva/iStockphoto.com
Back cover: © Sarsmis/iStockphoto.com; © OhlaAfanasieva

The Countryman Press
www.countrymanpress.com

A division of W. W. Norton & Company, Inc.,
500 Fifth Avenue, New York, NY 10110
www.wwnorton.com

For information about special discounts for bulk purchases, please contact W. W. Norton Special Sales at specialsales@wwnorton.com or 800-233-4830.

Printed in the United States

Library of Congress Cataloging-in-Publication Data

Sweeney, Monica.
  Best side dishes ever : foolproof recipes for greens, potatoes, beans, rice and more / Monica Sweeney.
    pages cm
Includes index.
ISBN 978-1-58157-322-0 (pbk.)
1. Side Dishes (Cooking)   I. Title.

TX740.S944 2015
641.81—dc23
                    2015018292

10 9 8 7 6 5 4 3 2 1

TO KATIE SWEENEY,
FOR SEA SALT AND
ROASTED VEGETABLES.

BEST SIDE DISHES EVER
CONTENTS

INTRODUCTION / 9

Chapter One: Salads / 11

Kohlrabi Slaw

Beet and Arugula Salad

Caprese Salad

Vegetable Orzo Pasta Salad

Crunchy Bok Choy Salad

Cous Cous Salad

Wheat Berry & Spinach Salad

Chapter Two: Vegetables / 27

Garlicky Green Beans

Creamed Spinach

Roasted Eggplant and
Pepper Mélange

Lemon-Pistachio Swiss Chard

Roasted Vegetable Medley

Roasted Artichoke

Balsamic Brussels Sprouts

Lemony Asparagus

Pine Nut Broccoli Rabe

Grilled Mexican Corn

Sun-Dried Tomato Broccoli

Bok Choy

Baked Veggie Fries

Chickpeas with Spinach
& Bacon

Ratatouille

Walnut Carrots

Chapter Three: Rice, Grains, & Pasta / 63

Mushroom Risotto

Pork Fried Rice

Sautéed Asparagus & Quinoa

Orecchiette with Peas

Three Cheese Risotto

Colby Jack Macaroni
and Cheese

Pumpkin Quinoa

Parmesan Polenta with
Sautéed Mushrooms

Chapter Four: Potato-Esque / 85

Crispy Potato Pancakes

Cranberry-Walnut Acorn Squash

Horseradish Mashed Potatoes

Spicy Jicama Fries

Thyme Sweet Potatoes

Potato Gratin

Tortilla Española

Chapter Five: Casseroles & Classics / 101

Cheese Soufflé

Tomatoes Provencal

Baked Beans

Vegetable Gratin

Popovers

Zucchini Casserole

Polenta Pizza

Vegetable-Stuffed Mushrooms

Cheesy Cauliflower

Rosemary Crispy Onions

Broccoli Quiche

Galette Ratatouille

INDEX / 127

Introduction

When a protein and two side dishes is standard fare for most meals, making dinner can lead to a lot of monotony. It's easy to focus on the main dish, whether it is a roasted chicken, a freshly grilled piece of seafood, or a juicy steak, but as a result, the sides are often left for dead, acting as filler in between bites of meat.

The array of recipes in this book runs the gamut: from incredibly simple arrangements with just a few ingredients that are bursting with fresh flavor, to more sophisticated medleys of spices, techniques, and ingredients that lead to incomparable taste. This book celebrates the side dish, from fresh roasted vegetables, to casseroles, to invigorating salads that will become the best part of every meal.

Whether you are a skilled home cook or just beginning, these recipes have been shaped to yield the very best flavors without being needlessly complicated. Try these recipes out on your family, friends, or just yourself, and watch how the sideshow of most meals can be as good as the main event.

CHAPTER ONE
SALADS

Kohlrabi Slaw

Coleslaw is often relegated to summer barbecues and as the tagalong of cornbread. This slaw uses fresh kohlrabi and a light, lemony vinaigrette instead of the standard sugary mayonnaise. If you can't find kohlrabi, try it with jicama, turnips, or another fresh and crisp vegetable.

Yield: 4–6 servings

1 cup kohlrabi, grated

1 cup carrots, grated

2 cups green cabbage, shredded

2 tablespoons lemon juice

3 tablespoons extra-virgin olive oil

½ tablespoon honey

½ tablespoon brown mustard

Pinch of salt and freshly ground black pepper

¼ cup scallions, sliced

Toss kohlrabi, carrots, and cabbage together in a large bowl. In a small bowl, make the dressing by whisking the lemon juice, olive oil, honey, mustard, salt, and pepper. Toss dressing with slaw, garnish with scallions, and serve chilled.

"There is no love sincerer than the love of food."
—George Bernard Shaw

Beet and Arugula Salad

Fresh, sweet beets and peppery arugula are the perfect match. With a light lemony dressing, crunchy walnuts, and creamy goat cheese, this salad has it all. Serve this salad as a side or top it with some protein for a whole meal.

Yield: 2 servings

- 3 medium beets
- ¼ cup balsamic vinegar
- 1 tablespoon lemon juice
- 3 tablespoons shallots, thinly sliced
- 1 tablespoon honey
- ⅓ cup extra-virgin olive oil
- Salt and freshly ground black pepper
- 6 cups fresh arugula
- ½ cup walnuts, toasted, chopped
- 3 ounces goat cheese, crumbled

Preheat the oven to 450°F. Loosely wrap beets in foil and bake for 30 to 35 minutes and set aside to cool. Peel and cut into slices. Whisk the vinegar, lemon juice, shallots, and honey together in a bowl. Blend the oil in gradually and season with salt and pepper. Toss the arugula, walnuts, and beets with the dressing. Plate and top with goat cheese.

Caprese Salad

There is nothing like a fresh mozzarella, tomato, and basil salad. Made of fresh ingredients that instinctively belong together, you can prepare it in just about any manner and it will automatically come out incredible. Mix together this dressing and drizzle over the mozzarella and tomato for an undeniably beautiful salad.

Yield: 2 servings

1 lemon, juiced

1 tablespoon red wine vinegar

1 small clove garlic, minced

Pinch of salt and freshly ground black pepper

⅓ cup extra-virgin olive oil

1 cup fresh cherry tomatoes, halved

1 cup mozzarella pearls, drained

½ cup basil leaves

Whisk lemon juice, vinegar, garlic, salt, pepper, and olive oil together until evenly blended. Toss dressing with tomatoes and mozzarella. Garnish with basil leaves.

"First we eat, then we do everything else."

—M. F. K. Fisher

Vegetable Orzo Pasta Salad

Is your old pasta salad recipe due for an update? Put the elbow macaroni back into the cupboard and try this fresh-tasting recipe using orzo, crisp veggies, and fresh herbs. The homemade vinaigrette is a cinch, and your modern twist on this classic will be ready in no time!

Yield: 8 servings

¼ cup red wine vinegar

2 tablespoons fresh lemon juice

½ cup olive oil

¼ teaspoon oregano

¼ teaspoon garlic powder

Pinch of salt and freshly ground black pepper

6 cups chicken broth

1 pound orzo

2 cups grape tomatoes

1 cup broccoli florets, blanched

1½ cups feta cheese

½ cup Kalamata olives

1 cup fresh basil, chopped

1 cup chopped green onions

½ cup pine nuts, toasted

To make vinaigrette, whisk vinegar and lemon juice together in small bowl, slowly adding in oil. Season with oregano, garlic powder, salt, and pepper. In a large saucepan, bring broth to a boil. Add in orzo and lower heat to medium,

partially covered. Cook for 5 to 7 minutes, or until tender. Drain and toss until cool. Once cooled, add tomatoes, broccoli, feta, olives, basil, green onions, and pine nuts until blended evenly. Toss with vinaigrette and serve.

Crunchy Bok Choy Salad

This fresh salad is full of surprises. Broken pieces of ramen sprinkled on top make for an interesting and fun way to liven up the texture, and freshly spiralized zucchini noodles pair well with the bok choy. If you don't have a tool for spiralizing, you can shred the zucchini with a box grater.

Yield: 2 servings

1 package dry ramen, broken into small pieces

2 tablespoons + 4 tablespoons vegetable oil, divided

1 teaspoon spicy chili sauce, such as Sriracha

¼ teaspoon honey

1 teaspoon peanut butter

1½ teaspoons toasted sesame oil

2 oranges, juiced

Pinch of salt and freshly ground black pepper

1 head bok choy, thinly sliced crosswise

1 red pepper, diced

1 zucchini, spiralized or shredded to make noodles

Preheat oven to 400°F. Break ramen into pieces and toss with 2 tablespoons of oil. (Do not use the flavor packet.) Bake or toast for 5 minutes or until lightly browned. Set aside. Whisk together chili sauce, honey, peanut butter, 4 tablespoons vegetable oil, sesame oil, orange juice, salt, and pepper. Toss dressing with bok choy, red pepper, and zucchini noodles. Sprinkle with toasted ramen pieces.

Cous Cous Salad

A bright and summery salad with the reviving flavors of pomegranate and lime, this is the medley to go along with fresh fish or grilled chicken. For a no-fuss way to remove the pomegranate seeds for this salad, halve and soak the fruit in water. After a few minutes, tap the peel vigorously with a wooden spoon over the bowl of water.

Yield: 8 servings

2 cups water

2 cups cous cous

⅓ cup extra-virgin olive oil

2 cloves garlic, minced

1 pomegranate, seeded

1 cup dried cranberries

½ cup mint leaves, chopped

½ cup parsley, chopped

2 tablespoons sesame seeds, toasted

Juice of 1 lime

Salt and pepper to taste

In a heat-safe bowl, pour boiling water over cous cous. Cover and let sit for 5 minutes while water absorbs. Fluff with fork and let cool. Toss with other ingredients and serve.

"Food is symbolic of love when words are inadequate."

—Alan D. Wolfelt

Wheat Berry & Spinach Salad

Tender, chewy wheat berries are not lauded as a fan favorite, but they certainly should be. You can prepare them in much the same way as cous cous, quinoa, or brown rice, and their added crunch makes them perfect for incorporating with salads. This robust salad takes on a whole host of flavors and textures that is endlessly pleasant.

Yield: 4 servings

½ cup wheat berries

½ cup quinoa

10 cups baby spinach

½ cup dried cranberries

1 yellow pepper, diced

½ cup green onion, chopped

⅓ cup sliced almonds, toasted

⅓ cup pine nuts, toasted

LEMON VINAIGRETTE

1 teaspoon finely grated lemon zest

4 tablespoons freshly squeezed lemon juice

1 teaspoon Dijon mustard

6 tablespoons extra-virgin olive oil

Pinch of salt and freshly ground black pepper

Add wheat berries to a pot and fill water to 2 inches above their surface. Bring to a boil and cook, uncovered, for 1 hour or until tender. Add quinoa to a different pot and bring to a boil with 1 cup of water. Once boiling, reduce the

heat and let simmer for 15 to 20 minutes, or until water is absorbed. Allow wheat berries and quinoa to cool. Toss all of the ingredients together. Whisk the vinaigrette ingredients together. Add vinaigrette until the salad has desired amount of dressing.

CHAPTER TWO

VEGETABLES

Garlicky Green Beans

Crisp green beans can be served with nearly any meal, whether it's fresh and lemony seafood or a rosemary tenderloin. This recipe is modest because the garden-fresh flavor of green beans needs no frills to be absolutely delectable.

Yield: 4 servings

1 pound green beans

2 tablespoons extra-virgin olive oil

2 cloves garlic, sliced

Pinch of salt and freshly ground black pepper

½ teaspoon crushed red pepper

Boil water in a large saucepan, and then add the green beans. Cook for 3 to 4 minutes or until al dente. Strain and set aside. Heat olive oil and garlic on medium heat for about 1 minute or until aromatic. Add the green beans, salt, and black pepper and stir until combined and hot. Sprinkle with crushed red pepper and serve hot.

Creamed Spinach

Creamed spinach tends to go underappreciated, but it's a true side dish gem. While many people prepare this dish with frozen spinach and canned mushrooms and throw it in the oven, using fresh ingredients can be just as easy and the results are far superior. For some additional texture, add crispy onions to the top prior to serving.

Yield: 4 servings

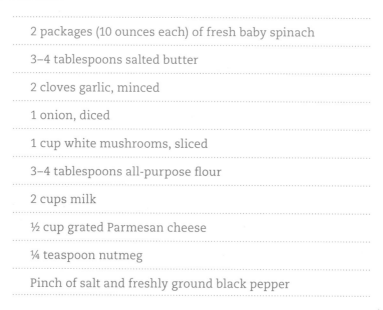

2 packages (10 ounces each) of fresh baby spinach

3–4 tablespoons salted butter

2 cloves garlic, minced

1 onion, diced

1 cup white mushrooms, sliced

3–4 tablespoons all-purpose flour

2 cups milk

½ cup grated Parmesan cheese

¼ teaspoon nutmeg

Pinch of salt and freshly ground black pepper

Blanch spinach in a pot of boiling water for 1 minute. Drain and transfer spinach to a bowl of cold water to stop the cooking process. Drain and squeeze excess water from the cooked spinach with a clean, dry kitchen towel. Chop the spinach and remove large stems. Set aside. Melt butter in a saucepan and add the garlic, onion, and mushrooms. Cook until tender or the onions are translucent. Stir in the flour until the mixture becomes a paste, then stir in the milk to thicken. Stir in the Parmesan, nutmeg, and then the spinach. Season with salt and pepper and serve.

> "We all eat, and it would be a sad waste of opportunity to eat badly."
> —Anna Thomas

Roasted Eggplant and Pepper Mélange

A lemony blend of summer vegetables, this roasted dish puts the rich color and flavor of eggplant at center stage. This assortment of flavors goes seamlessly with shrimp or chicken right off the grill.

Yield: 4–6 servings

2 large eggplants peeled, cut into 1½-inch chunks

1½ tablespoons salt

2 red peppers, chopped into large chunks

¼ cup extra-virgin olive oil

½ medium shallot, finely chopped

2 cloves garlic, minced

½ teaspoon freshly ground pepper

2 tablespoons walnut oil

½ cup parsley

2 teaspoons lemon juice

Preheat the oven to 425°F. Sprinkle eggplant with 1½ tablespoons salt and let drain in a strainer for 20 minutes. Toss the eggplant and red peppers with the olive oil, shallots, garlic, and black pepper. Arrange evenly on a foil or parchment-lined baking sheet. Roast for about 30 minutes, or until tender but not overcooked. Remove from the oven and stir in the walnut oil, parsley, and lemon juice.

Lemon-Pistachio Swiss Chard

This zesty combination of leafy greens, crunchy pistachios, and lemon doesn't trade flavor for nutrition. Incredibly delicious, you won't want to cook up your greens in any other way.

Yield: 2 servings

2 tablespoons butter

2 tablespoons olive oil

1 tablespoon garlic, minced

1 bunch Swiss chard, chopped and stems separated

½ cup dry white wine

½ cup shelled pistachio nuts, coarsely chopped

Juice of 1 lemon

2 tablespoons Parmesan

Melt the butter and olive oil in a skillet. Add the garlic and heat on medium heat for about 1 minute or until aromatic. Stir in the stems and the white wine and let simmer for 5 minutes. Add the Swiss chard leaves and heat until wilted. Add pistachio nuts, lemon juice, and Parmesan until evenly coated.

"I cook with wine. Sometimes I even add it to the food."

—W. C. Fields

Roasted Vegetable Medley

Sprinkle your favorite vegetables with some rosemary, salt, freshly cracked pepper, and a drizzle of great olive oil for the most perfect expression of natural flavors. This no-frills recipe showcases just how simple, fresh ingredients can be equal to—if not better than—some of the most extravagant recipes.

Yield: 4–6 servings

½ head cauliflower

½ head broccoli

6 carrots, peeled

1 medium red onion, peeled and chopped

3 tablespoons extra-virgin olive oil

½ teaspoon dried rosemary

½ teaspoon oregano

2 teaspoons salt

1 teaspoon freshly ground black pepper

Preheat the oven to 400°F. Break cauliflower and broccoli down into florets. Discard larger stems. Cut large carrots into halves or quarters, lengthwise, and leave smaller carrots whole. Toss vegetables with olive oil, rosemary, oregano, salt, and pepper. Arrange in a cast-iron pan or on a parchment- or foil-lined baking sheet. Roast in the oven for 25 minutes, or until tender and slightly browned.

Roasted Artichoke

This roasted artichoke is simple and delicious, complemented by a little bit of lemon and a lot of garlic. Preparation involves very little effort, and the payoff is tenfold. For those who have never eaten an artichoke in whole form before, just tear off the leaves and scrape off the meaty bits with your teeth to enjoy a mouthwatering and healthy supplement to your meal.

Yield: 2 servings

2 artichokes

1 lemon

2 tablespoons extra-virgin olive oil

Pinch of salt and freshly ground black pepper

6 garlic cloves

Preheat oven to 425°F. Prepare the artichokes by cutting off the bottom stems and very tops. Hollow out the center leaves to make room for the garlic, and spread the rest of the leaves out. Squeeze half a lemon and drizzle 1 tablespoon of olive oil over each artichoke. Sprinkle with salt and pepper and fill the cavities with 3 garlic cloves each. Wrap artichokes individually with foil and roast for 1 hour, or until tender.

Balsamic Brussels Sprouts

You may remember the days when Brussels sprouts were typically boiled and served. These poor sprouts got a bad rap for being mushy and flavorless for too long. Thankfully times have changed in the kitchen and this side is not only packed with flavor, but Vitamin C and fiber, too!

Yield: 6 servings

1½ pounds Brussels sprouts

2 tablespoons + 1 tablespoon extra-virgin olive oil, divided

Pinch of salt and freshly ground black pepper

Juice of 1 lemon

1 teaspoon honey

1 tablespoon balsamic vinegar

Preheat oven to 425°F. Cut off Brussels sprout bases and any wilting leaves. Slice into halves for smaller sprouts and quarters for larger sprouts. Toss the sprouts with 2 tablespoons olive oil, salt, and pepper. Arrange on a parchment- or foil-lined baking sheet and cook for 20 to 25 minutes, or until crispy. Place cooked sprouts in a bowl and toss with 1 tablespoon of olive oil, lemon juice, honey, and balsamic vinegar until dressed evenly.

"Food is everything we are. It's an extension of nationalist feeling, ethnic feeling, your personal history, your province, your region, your tribe, your grandma. It's inseparable from those from the get-go." —Anthony Bourdain

Lemony Asparagus

Welcome in springtime with this simple asparagus dish you can toss together in minutes! Asparagus is a fantastic source of nutrients and vitamins and when sautéed with garlic and shallots and topped with Parmesan cheese, it's a stunning addition to your family table.

Yield: 2–4 servings

1 tablespoon olive oil

1 medium shallot, minced

1 clove garlic, minced

1 bunch fresh asparagus spears, trimmed

Juice of 1 lemon

Pinch of salt and freshly ground black pepper

¼ cup Parmesan cheese

Heat olive oil, shallots, and garlic on medium heat for about 1 minute or until aromatic. Add asparagus and cook for 5 minutes, or until tender and slightly browned. Remove from heat and season with lemon juice, salt, and pepper, and top with cheese.

Pine Nut Broccoli Rabe

Sometimes known as rapini, broccoli rabe is the slightly peppery vegetable that has everything. With a little added crunch from the toasted pine nuts, this can go with just about any meal, from fresh-roasted fish to a hearty steak.

Yield: 4–6 servings

4 bunches broccoli rabe, stems trimmed

2 tablespoons pine nuts, toasted

¼ cup olive oil

3 garlic cloves, chopped

½ teaspoon crushed red pepper flakes

Pinch of salt and freshly ground black pepper

Blanch broccoli rabe in a pot of boiling water for 1 minute. Drain and transfer to a bowl of cold water to stop the cooking process, reserving ¼ cup of cooking water. Drain the broccoli rabe and set aside. In a pan or toaster oven, toast the pine nuts for 2 to 3 minutes or until lightly browned. Heat olive oil and garlic on medium heat for about 1 minute or until aromatic. Reduce to low heat and add broccoli rabe, stirring until mixed with garlic and oil. Add the cooking water and cook for 4 to 5 minutes or until tender. Toss with toasted pine nuts and red pepper flakes and season with salt and pepper prior to serving.

"He who distinguishes the true savor of his food can never be a glutton; he who does not cannot be otherwise."   —Henry David Thoreau

Grilled Mexican Corn

There's nothing like fresh, sweet corn in the summertime. While corn is delicious with some butter and salt, the added flavors of chili powder and tangy lime really give it extra star power.

Yield: 4 ears

4 ears corn

1 tablespoon salt

½ cup mayonnaise

1 ½ cups sour cream

½ teaspoon celery salt

¼ cup freshly chopped cilantro leaves

1 lime, juiced

1 cup freshly grated Parmesan (optional)

Red chili powder, to taste

Preheat the grill to medium. Pull down the cornhusks without detaching. Remove the silk and fold the husks back over the corn. Let sit in water with 1 tablespoon of salt for 10 minutes. Dry off the corn and grill for 15 to 20 minutes, turning periodically to cook all sides. Mix the mayonnaise, sour cream, celery salt, and cilantro. Remove the husks and lather the corn with the mayonnaise mixture. Squeeze lime juice over the corn and then sprinkle liberally with Parmesan. Finish with chili powder and serve.

Sun-Dried Tomato Broccoli

Cutting back on carbs doesn't have to mean cutting back on flavor. Complete your healthy meal with this delicious vegetable dish with the tangy taste of balsamic vinegar providing an excellent source of antioxidants while broccoli serves up plenty of Vitamin C!

Yield: 4–6 servings

1 head broccoli

3 tablespoons extra-virgin olive oil

1 clove garlic, finely chopped

3 tablespoons balsamic vinegar

Pinch of salt and freshly ground black pepper

¼ cup sliced sun-dried tomatoes

Break broccoli down into florets. Discard larger stems. Cook broccoli in a pot of boiling water or steam with a vegetable steamer for about 3 minutes or until bright green. Heat olive oil and garlic on medium heat for about 1 minute or until aromatic. In a small bowl, combine balsamic vinegar, garlic, olive oil, salt, and pepper. Add sun-dried tomatoes, broccoli, and balsamic dressing and toss until evenly coated.

Bok Choy

Bok choy is perpetually given a supporting role to most dishes instead of the lead. This crisp, slightly bitter green is a delicious mealtime component, especially when prepared with the right blend of lively ingredients. With a little bit of ginger, soy sauce, and garlic, this tangy recipe brings out the very best aspects of this show-stopping veggie.

Yield: 4–6 servings

½ tablespoon olive oil

½ tablespoon sesame oil

1 tablespoon minced fresh ginger

2 cloves garlic, minced

1 tablespoon rice wine vinegar

4 heads bok choy, whole or chopped

2 tablespoons soy sauce

Pinch of salt and freshly ground black pepper

Heat olive oil, sesame oil, ginger, and garlic on medium heat for about 1 minute or until aromatic. Add vinegar, bok choy, and soy sauce, cooking for 5 minutes or until the greens have wilted. Season with salt and pepper to taste.

Baked Veggie Fries

Who said fries couldn't be colorful and bright? These veggie fries add extra layers of excitement both in flavor and in appearance that regular potato fries just don't have. Just like veggie chips, these fries are a healthier alternative to liven up any meal.

Yield: 8 servings

½ pound beets

½ pound carrots

½ pound parsnips

2 tablespoons parsley, finely chopped

¼ cup olive oil

Pinch of salt and freshly ground black pepper

Preheat oven to 400°F. Clean and peel the vegetables thoroughly and trim stems. Slice into strips, about 3 to 4 inches in length depending on preference. Cover evenly with parsley, olive oil, salt, and pepper. Arrange vegetable fries evenly on a parchment- or foil-lined baking sheet. Bake for 20 to 25 minutes, or until the desired crispiness.

"Dinner is not what you do in the evening before something else. Dinner is the evening."   —Art Buchwald

Chickpeas with Spinach & Bacon

You'll be hard pressed to find someone turning down this side dish! Savory bacon pairs beautifully with hearty chickpeas and healthful spinach in this flavorful and colorful combo that rounds out a summertime barbecue. Try it at your next gathering!

Yield: 4 servings

3 slices bacon

3 tablespoons extra-virgin olive oil

1 (15-ounce) can chickpeas, rinsed

¼ teaspoon crushed red pepper

1 teaspoon red wine vinegar

8 cups baby spinach

1 garlic clove, minced

Pinch of salt and freshly ground black pepper

Cook bacon in a skillet over medium-high until it is cooked through but not crispy. Remove from pan and cut into bits. Drain bacon grease, leaving coating of grease on the skillet. Return the bacon bits to the pan. Add oil, chickpeas, and red pepper flakes to the skillet, over high heat. Stir the mixture for 3 to 4 minutes or until chickpeas begin to lightly brown. Add vinegar, spinach, and garlic and cook until the spinach is wilted. Season with salt and pepper to taste and serve.

Ratatouille

A summer in Provence is at your table with this fresh dish. A beautiful blend of seasonal vegetables that have been slow cooked and nurtured with subtle spices, ratatouille is the delightful, nourishing accompaniment to meals that can make you feel like you're in the rolling hills of France.

Yield: 4 servings

1 (28-ounce) can whole peeled tomatoes

2 tablespoons + 4 tablespoons extra-virgin olive oil, divided

1 large eggplant, chopped into chunks

1 tablespoon salt

2 large yellow onions, diced

1 head garlic, peeled and minced

2 bell peppers, seeded and chopped

1 large zucchini, chopped

1 large summer squash, chopped

1 teaspoon dried basil

1 bay leaf

1 tablespoon oregano

1 tablespoon minced rosemary, plus sprigs for garnish

2–3 tablespoons red wine vinegar

Pinch of salt and freshly ground black pepper

Preheat oven to 350°F. Pour can of tomatoes (including juices) onto a rimmed baking sheet. Break tomatoes into smaller pieces and mix in 2 tablespoons of olive oil. Bake for 30 minutes, stirring occasionally, until thickened. While the tomatoes cook, toss eggplant with 1 tablespoon salt and let drain in a strainer for 20 minutes. In a large pot, heat 4 tablespoons olive oil over medium-high.

Stir in onion and cook for a few minutes until translucent. Add garlic, stirring for another 5 minutes. Stir in peppers, cooking for another 5 minutes or until tender. Add tomatoes, eggplant, zucchini, squash, basil, bay leaf, and oregano to pot and stir until it reaches a simmer. Lower the heat to medium-low and cook, partially covered, for about 15 minutes. Do not overcook. Stir in minced rosemary and vinegar. Season with salt and pepper before serving.

Walnut Carrots

There is no more perfect way to cook carrots than this simple recipe. With a little bit of salt to bring out their natural sweetness and chopped walnuts to add an extra crunch, these roasted carrots are sure to be a side dish staple.

Yield: 2 servings

12 carrots, peeled

3 tablespoons extra-virgin olive oil

2 teaspoons salt

1 teaspoon freshly ground black pepper

½ teaspoon dried thyme

½ cup chopped walnuts

Preheat the oven to 400°F. Cut large carrots into halves or quarters, lengthwise, and leave smaller carrots whole. Toss carrots with olive oil, salt, pepper, and thyme. Spread carrots out on a parchment- or foil-lined baking sheet. Roast in the oven for 25 minutes, or until tender and slightly browned. Sprinkle with thyme and chopped walnuts when ready to serve.

CHAPTER THREE

RICE, GRAINS, & PASTA

Mushroom Risotto

This scrumptious risotto dish is nothing if not comforting. The Arborio rice is the benchmark for this recipe, but you can swap it out with barley and brown rice as well. With enriching chicken broth and hearty mushrooms, this preparation is good enough to be a whole meal.

Yield: 6 servings

6 cups chicken broth

3 tablespoons olive oil, divided

1 cup Portobello mushrooms, thinly sliced

1 cup white mushrooms, thinly sliced

1 cup shiitake mushrooms, thinly sliced

2 shallots, diced

2 cloves garlic, minced

1½ cups Arborio rice

½ cup dry white wine

4 tablespoons butter

⅓ cup Parmesan, grated

3 tablespoons parsley, chopped

Pinch of salt and freshly ground black pepper

Warm the chicken broth in a saucepan over low heat. In a separate, large skillet, heat 2 tablespoons of olive oil over medium-high. Add the mushrooms to the same skillet, and cook for 2 to 3 minutes or until tender. Remove the mushrooms and set aside. Add another tablespoon of olive oil to the same skillet and then add the shallots and garlic. Cook until warmed, and then slowly stir in the rice for about 2 minutes. Pour in white wine, stirring to coat the rice evenly until absorbed. Ladle in chicken broth ½ cup at a time, stirring constantly. Wait until each addition is absorbed before ladling in more. After 15 to 20 minutes when all the broth is fully absorbed, remove the risotto from the burner. Fold in mushrooms, butter, and Parmesan. Garnish with parsley and sprinkle with salt and pepper.

Pork Fried Rice

Most often associated with heavy, salty takeout, this dish takes away all the guilt. Making pork fried rice at home is easy, and you don't have to worry about unknown added ingredients. The pork can be swapped with shrimp, chicken, beef, or the extra vegetables you have on hand to make it just the way you like it.

Yield: 4 servings

6 cups short-grain rice, cooked

4 large eggs, lightly beaten

3 tablespoons soy sauce

5 teaspoons rice vinegar

1 tablespoon sesame oil

¼ teaspoon sugar

¼ cup vegetable shortening

¾ pound Chinese barbecued pork, cut into pieces

½ cup peas

2 shiitake mushrooms, sliced and stems removed

1 carrot, diced

1 head baby bok choy, chopped

2 cloves garlic, minced

2 scallions, thinly sliced

Pinch of salt and freshly ground black pepper

¼ cup pickled ginger

Cook rice according to package instructions. Set aside. Scramble eggs and set aside. Mix the soy sauce, rice vinegar, sesame oil, and sugar in a ramekin or small bowl. Melt vegetable shortening in a large skillet over medium heat. Increase the heat to medium-high and add the pork, cooking for 1 minute. Stir in the peas, mushrooms, carrots, and bok choy, cooking for 3 to 4 minutes or until tender. Add garlic and cook another minute. Fold in the eggs. Fold in the rice, scallions, and sauce and cook until the mixture is heated through. Season with salt and pepper prior to serving. Garnish with pickled ginger.

Tip: If you have picky eaters at the table, sauté the vegetables in batches, and skip the egg altogether. That way you can offer individual bowls of cooked ingredients, and each person can create their own fried rice bowl.

"I like rice. Rice is great if you're hungry and want 2,000 of something."
— Mitch Hedberg

Sautéed Asparagus & Quinoa

Hearty quinoa and fresh asparagus make for an unpretentious but tasty comple-ment to a meal. This recipe calls for chicken broth to add a hint of savory goodness, but you can also use water to make the fluffy quinoa. The lemony asparagus is just the right touch for a clean-tasting and healthy side dish.

Yield: 4–6 servings

- 1 cup quinoa
- ½ tablespoon + 1½ tablespoons olive oil, divided
- 2 cups chicken broth
- 1 medium shallot, diced
- 1 pound fresh asparagus, cut in pieces with ends removed
- 1 red bell pepper, cored and diced
- 2 cloves garlic, minced
- ¼ teaspoon oregano
- 1 teaspoon lemon juice
- Pinch of salt and freshly ground black pepper

In a fine-mesh strainer, rinse the quinoa under cold water. Shake out excess water. Heat ½ tablespoon of olive oil in a saucepan over medium-high. Add the quinoa, stirring occasionally, and cook for 1 minute or until lightly toasted. Pour in broth and bring to a boil. Reduce the heat to a light simmer and cook, covered, for 15 minutes or until the water is absorbed. While the quinoa is cooking, heat remaining olive oil on high in a sauté pan and cook shallots until barely translucent. Add the asparagus, red pepper, garlic, oreg-ano, lemon juice, salt, and pepper and cook until the asparagus are al dente. Remove the quinoa from the heat and let stand as is for 5 minutes. Fluff with a fork and stir in asparagus mixture.

Orecchiette with Peas

Orecchiette comes from the Italian word for "little ears," which is a cute description for a delightful little pasta. If you can't find orecchiette, medium-sized pasta shells are a good alternative. Stir this in with the fresh peas and some salty prosciutto, and you have a decadent addition to a meal in just a few minutes.

Yield: 4 servings

8 ounces orecchiette pasta

1½ teaspoons kosher salt

3 tablespoons olive oil

3 cloves garlic, minced or grated

1 cup peas, fresh or thawed

1 cup crème fraîche

¼ cup Parmesan cheese

6 slices prosciutto, shredded

12 small basil leaves, or 6 large ones roughly torn

In a large pot, bring water to a boil. Add pasta and a sprinkle of salt, cooking until pasta is al dente. While the pasta cooks, heat olive oil and garlic on medium heat for about 1 minute or until aromatic. Stir in the peas, then add the crème fraîche and salt. Bring to a simmer and continue to stir until heated through. Drain the pasta, reserving ⅓ cup of the cooking water, and add the pasta to the saucepan. Once the pasta is blended with the sauce, add the ⅓ cup of cooking water and cheese. Increase the heat to high and cook for 2 to 3 more minutes. Stir in the prosciutto and basil leaves.

> "Life is a combination of magic and pasta."
>
> —Federico Fellini

Three Cheese Risotto

Risotto may seem like a complex dish that can only be ordered in a restaurant, but this simple recipe lets you create the traditions of Italian comfort food at home. With three different cheeses topped with fresh lemon and chopped chives, your taste buds will be so pleased.

Yield: 4–6 servings

6 cups chicken broth

2 tablespoon olive oil

1 cup shallots, chopped

2 teaspoons chopped garlic

1½ cups Arborio rice

½ cup dry white wine

Juice of 1 lemon

4 tablespoons butter

¼ cup Pecorino cheese, grated

¼ cup Parmesan cheese, grated

¼ cup Asiago cheese, grated

1 teaspoon parsley, chopped

Pinch of salt and freshly ground black pepper

Warm the chicken broth in a saucepan over low heat. In a separate, large skillet, heat the olive oil over medium-high, add the shallots and garlic. Cook until warmed, and then slowly stir in the rice for about 2 minutes. Pour in white wine and lemon juice, stirring to coat the rice evenly until absorbed. Ladle in chicken broth ½ cup at a time, stirring constantly. Wait until each addition is absorbed before ladling in more. After 15 to 20 minutes when all the broth is fully absorbed, fold in butter and three cheeses. Garnish with parsley, salt, and pepper and serve immediately.

Colby Jack Macaroni and Cheese

All mac 'n' cheeses are not created equal, and this one comes out on top. The blend of sharp cheddar and Colby jack cheeses makes for incomparable taste, and the added buttery bread crumbs will have everyone eager for seconds.

Yield: 4–6 servings

4 cups medium shell macaroni

4 tablespoons butter

4 tablespoons flour

2 cups milk

Pinch of salt and freshly ground black pepper

6 cups sharp cheddar, shredded

2 cups Colby jack, cubed

½ cup sour cream

½ cup Italian bread crumbs

Preheat oven to 350°F. In a large pot, bring water to a boil. Add pasta and a sprinkle of salt, cooking until pasta is al dente. In a separate, large saucepan, create a roux by melting the butter and gradually adding in flour. Slowly add the milk, salt, and pepper on medium-low heat until thickened. Sprinkle in the cheddar while stirring continuously. Wait for cheese to melt before adding more. Reserve ½ cup for sprinkling at the end. Add sour cream. Mix in the pasta shells until evenly coated. Pour the shells into a large baking dish in layers. Add Colby jack cheese to each layer. Finish with cheddar as the top layer and sprinkle bread crumbs liberally. Bake for 45 to 55 minutes or until lightly browned.

Tip: Can also be cooked in small tapas dishes. Cut time in half.

Pumpkin Quinoa

What better way to welcome the autumn months than introducing pumpkin to your favorite dishes? As the seasons change and the air turns brisk and chilly, warm up with this flavorful hearty combination.

Yield: 2–4 servings

1 cup water

1 cup coconut milk

1 cup quinoa

½ cup pumpkin puree

½ teaspoon ginger

1 teaspoon cinnamon

½ teaspoon cloves

Pinch of salt

½ cup fresh pumpkin, cubed

Bring water and coconut milk to a boil. Add the quinoa, pumpkin puree, ginger, cinnamon, cloves, and salt. Reduce the heat and cook for 10 minutes or until the liquid has absorbed. Place the fresh pumpkin in a microwave-safe bowl, covered, with 1 tablespoon of water. Cook on high for 5 to 7 minutes, or until pumpkin is fork tender. Remove the quinoa from heat and top with cooked fresh pumpkin.

Parmesan Polenta with Sautéed Mushrooms

Creamy polenta and garlicky mushrooms work together for an incredible addition to a meal that is wholesome and filling. The polenta is enhanced with the savory chicken broth and Parmesan, resulting in an amazing, velvety texture.

Yield: 2 servings

POLENTA

4 cups chicken broth

2 cloves garlic, minced

1 cup polenta or yellow stone-ground cornmeal

1 tablespoon salt

1 teaspoon freshly ground black pepper

¼ cup crème fraîche

1 cup freshly grated Parmesan cheese

2 tablespoons (¼ stick) unsalted butter

SAUTÉED MUSHROOMS

2 tablespoons olive oil

3 cloves garlic, chopped

12 ounces baby Portobello mushrooms, thinly sliced

½ teaspoon dried, ground sage

Pinch of salt and freshly ground black pepper

1 teaspoon Parmesan

2 tablespoons parsley, chopped

In a large saucepan, bring chicken broth and garlic to a boil over medium-high. Reduce the heat to medium-low and slowly add the cornmeal. Stir continuously with a whisk to break down clumps. Add salt and pepper and keep stirring for 10 minutes or until it thickens. Remove from heat and stir in crème fraîche, Parmesan, and butter. Keep warm on a double boiler while cooking the mushrooms. Heat olive oil and garlic on medium-high heat for about 1 minute or until aromatic. Add the mushrooms and a sprinkle of sage, salt, and pepper and cook for another 5 minutes or until lightly browned. Plate the polenta and top with the mushrooms. Sprinkle with Parmesan and parsley.

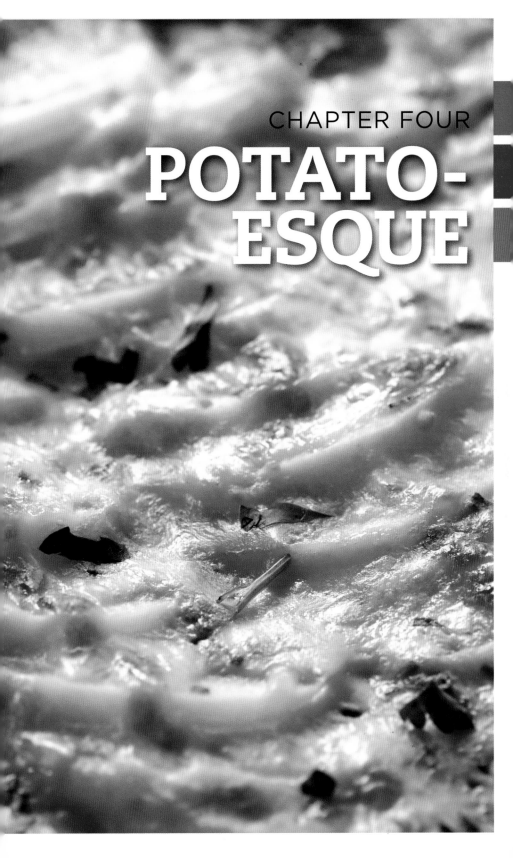

CHAPTER FOUR

POTATO-ESQUE

Crispy Potato Pancakes

Crispy and savory, these potato pancakes are classic for a reason. Whether you are putting in a little extra sweat and shredding the potatoes with a box grater or just tossing them into the food processor, the result is a comforting side for holiday traditions and weeknight meals alike.

Yield: 6 servings

1 pound russet potatoes, peeled (2–3 potatoes)

1 small onion

1 large egg, lightly beaten

¼ teaspoon garlic powder

3 tablespoons matzo meal

Pinch of salt and freshly ground black pepper

½ cup vegetable oil

1 tablespoon chives, snipped

Chop the potatoes into large pieces and soak in water for an hour. Coarsely shred the potatoes and onion in a food processor. On a clean, dry kitchen towel, press out any excess moisture from the shredded potatoes and onions. Add the potatoes and onions to a large bowl and stir in the egg, garlic powder, matzo meal, salt, and pepper. Heat the vegetable oil in a large skillet on medium-high. In batches, drop heaping tablespoons of the potatoes onto the pan, flattening them into 3–inch pancakes with a spoon or spatula. Cook for 3 to 4 minutes on each side, or until the pancakes have lightly browned. Sprinkle with chives and serve with sour cream or apple sauce.

Cranberry-Walnut Acorn Squash

Autumn eternal, this stuffed squash is as beautiful to serve as it is luscious and tasty. The elaborate presentation is deceiving, because this recipe is quite straight-forward and simple to prepare.

Yield: 2 servings

½ cup walnuts, roughly chopped

½ cup cranberries, fresh or thawed

4 tablespoons brown sugar

1 acorn squash, halved and seeded

2 tablespoons butter

Pinch of salt and freshly ground black pepper

Preheat the oven to 375°F. In a bowl, toss the walnuts, cranberries, and brown sugar until evenly mixed. Spoon the cranberry-walnut mixture into the cavities of the squash and top each half with 1 tablespoon of butter, salt, and pepper. Place squash in a baking dish and cover with foil. Bake for 1 hour and 25 minutes, or until fork goes into flesh easily. Remove the foil and broil for last minute to brown the top (optional).

"The most remarkable thing about my mother is that for thirty years she served the family nothing but leftovers. The original meal has never been found."

—Calvin Trillin

Horseradish Mashed Potatoes

Hot, buttery mashed potatoes taste like home, but this added kick takes them on an adventure. The flavor power of horseradish can go a long way, so using just a little will be enough to make this spin on traditional mashed potatoes an exciting departure from the gold standard.

Yield: 6 servings

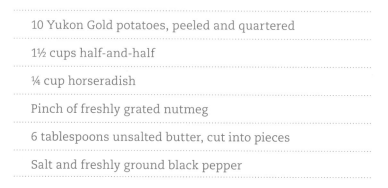

10 Yukon Gold potatoes, peeled and quartered

1½ cups half-and-half

¼ cup horseradish

Pinch of freshly grated nutmeg

6 tablespoons unsalted butter, cut into pieces

Salt and freshly ground black pepper

In a large pot of water, bring the potatoes to a boil over medium-high heat. Cook for 20 minutes or until tender. Heat the half-and-half, horseradish, and nutmeg in a small saucepan over medium-low heat. Bring to a light simmer but do not boil. Drain the potatoes and then put them through a ricer, food mill, or crush with a potato masher. Stir in the butter and horseradish-cream mixture, and season with salt and pepper.

"Laughter is brightest where food is best."

—Irish Proverb

Spicy Jicama Fries

Jicama, sometimes known as a Mexican turnip, gets very little airtime on the vegetable scene. This underdog is great in salads, stir-fry, and even on a standard crudité platter, but these crunchy fries let jicama really shine. If you aren't big on spice but want to steer from a typical order of French fries, cook them plain and then sprinkle with a little salt and pepper.

Yield: 3 servings

1 medium jicama

1 tablespoon coconut or vegetable oil

½ teaspoon cumin

½ teaspoon turmeric

½ teaspoon garlic powder

Pinch of salt and freshly ground black pepper

Pinch of cayenne or chili powder

Preheat oven to 400°F. Peel the jicama and slice into thin-cut fries. Pre-cook the jicama: Place the fries in a bowl with a tablespoon of water and micro-wave, covered with a damp paper towel, for 5 minutes. Drain the jicama and lightly pat dry. Toss the jicama fries with the oil and all of the spices. Arrange evenly on a parchment- or foil-lined baking sheet and bake for 40 minutes, or until they are lightly browned. Shift with a spatula or tongs at least once.

Thyme Sweet Potatoes

The crispy and sugary essence of sweet potatoes is a treat in itself, so this preparation takes a minimalist approach to let those flavors shine. With a little bit of spice from the red pepper and some fragrant thyme, these potatoes are like none other.

Yield: 6 servings

4 medium sweet potatoes, peeled and cut into cubes

3 tablespoons olive oil

4 large garlic cloves, minced

⅓ cup fresh thyme leaves

½ teaspoon kosher salt

½ teaspoon red pepper flakes

2 sprigs thyme for garnish

Preheat oven to 450°F. Toss ingredients together until sweet potatoes are evenly coated. Arrange on a parchment- or foil-lined baking sheet and roast for 45 minutes or until tender and lightly browned. Garnish with thyme sprigs.

"I hate people who are not serious about meals. It is so shallow of them."
—Oscar Wilde, *The Importance of Being Earnest*

Potato Gratin

A medley of simple ingredients that makes for a rich and creamy dish, these scalloped potatoes are more than what they seem. Whether you are taking all day to make rack of lamb or are whipping up something quickly, potato gratin can go with just about anything.

Yield: 6 servings

10 Idaho potatoes, peeled

2 tablespoons unsalted butter, softened

2 cloves garlic, minced

1½–2 cups half-and-half

Salt and freshly ground black pepper to taste

1 teaspoon nutmeg

½ cup heavy cream

½ cup Parmesan

Preheat the oven to 350°F. Slice potatoes to ⅛–inch thick using a sharp knife or mandolin. Using the butter, grease a shallow baking dish. Coat with half of minced garlic. In a saucepan, bring the half-and-half to a simmer over medium heat. Season with salt and pepper and add the rest of the garlic. Arrange the potatoes in one layer in the baking dish, overlapping like fish scales. Season this layer with salt, pepper, and nutmeg. Repeat this process in layers until all of the potatoes are gone or the dish is nearly filled. Pour the hot half-and-half over the potatoes, but do not fill above the top layer. Bake, covered, for 1 hour or until fork tender. Remove the foil and increase the heat to 415°F. Bake for another 8 to 10 minutes or until the potatoes are lightly browned. Pour cream over the top and sprinkle with parmesan. Bake for another 15 minutes or until the top is lightly browned. Remove from the oven and let stand for 10 minutes and serve.

Tortilla Española

A traditional *tapa* or small plate in Spain, this egg-and-potato side dish is heartier than a quiche or frittata. Perfecting this recipe can take time, but the results speak for themselves. Serve in small bites or in wedges.

Yield: 4 servings

4 strands saffron

½ cup extra-virgin olive oil

2 large baking potatoes, peeled and thinly sliced crosswise

1 cup red onion, thinly sliced

5 large eggs

½ cup fresh cilantro, chopped

1 tablespoon fresh thyme

¼ teaspoon paprika

¼ teaspoon cumin

Pinch of salt and freshly ground black pepper

2 tablespoons olive oil

Preheat oven to 400°F. In an 8-inch skillet, heat saffron and olive oil over medium heat. Stir in potatoes and onion. Add more oil if necessary so that they are completely covered. Reduce the heat to medium-low and cook for 20 minutes. Remove contents from the skillet and drain out the oil. Combine potato mixture with eggs, cilantro, thyme, paprika, cumin, salt, and pepper. Mix well. Heat 2 tablespoons of olive oil over medium heat. Pour in mixture and press down evenly. Reduce heat and cook, uncovered, for 4 to 5 minutes or until the bottom has lightly browned. Cover with a ceramic plate and flip the tortilla onto the plate. Slide the tortilla, uncooked side down, back into the skillet. Cook for another 4 to 5 minutes. Remove from pan and serve in slices.

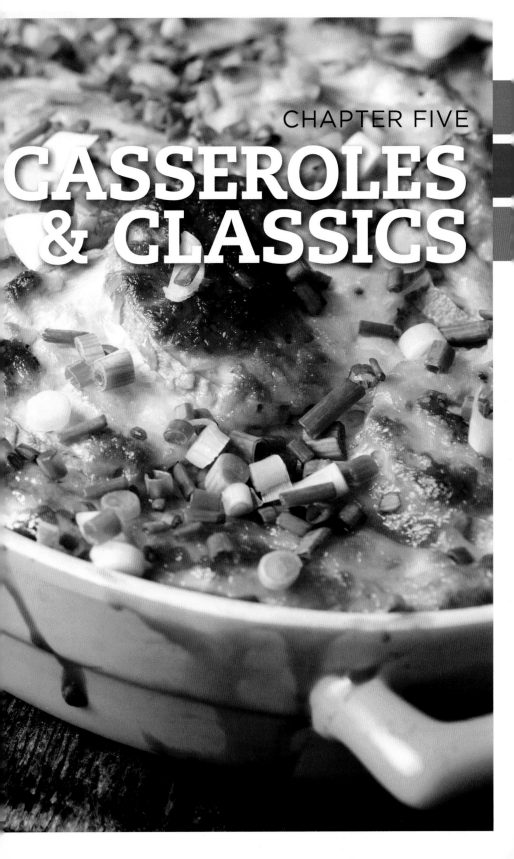

CHAPTER FIVE

CASSEROLES
& CLASSICS

Cheese Soufflé

Say bonjour to this delectable cheese soufflé! Your soiree guests will be wowed by your expertise and culinary prowess when you whip up this sumptuous dish for your next gathering with friends. A bold cabernet sauvignon pairs perfectly.

Yield: 4–6 servings

2 tablespoons Parmesan, grated

1 cup whole milk

2½ tablespoons unsalted butter

3 tablespoons all-purpose flour

½ teaspoon paprika

Pinch of ground nutmeg

½ teaspoon salt

4 large egg yolks

5 large egg whites

1 cup Gruyère cheese, grated

Preheat oven to 400°F. Grease a 1½-quart soufflé dish. Coat the dish with Parmesan cheese. In a small saucepan, heat milk over medium-low until steaming. In a large saucepan, melt butter over medium heat. Whisk in flour for about 3 minutes, but do not brown. Remove from heat and let stand for 1 minute. Whisk in milk and then return to heat, stirring for 2 to 3 minutes until thick. Remove from heat and stir in paprika, nutmeg, and salt. Whisk in egg yolks one at a time. Pour base into a large bowl and let cool to lukewarm. In a separate bowl, beat egg whites until stiff. Pour ¼ of the egg whites into soufflé base. Sprinkle in cheese and continue folding in the rest of the egg whites. Pour mixture into soufflé dish and place into the oven. Reduce the oven heat to 375°F. Bake for about 25 minutes or until the soufflé is puffy and golden. Do not open the oven door while monitoring it.

Tomatoes Provencal

These incredibly tasty stuffed tomatoes are inspired by Mediterranean cuisines that celebrate an array of fresh produce, herbs, and spices. This super-simple recipe can be thrown together for unexpected guests, making you look like the perfect host.

Yield: 8 servings

- 6 tomatoes, about 3 inches in diameter
- Pinch of salt and freshly ground black pepper
- 1½ cups bread crumbs
- ¼ cup minced scallions
- ¼ cup basil leaves, minced
- 2 cloves garlic, minced
- 2 tablespoons parsley, minced
- ½ teaspoon oregano
- 1 teaspoon salt
- ½ cup grated Gruyère cheese
- 2 tablespoon extra-virgin olive oil

Preheat the oven to 400°F. Cut tomatoes in half crosswise and gently remove the seeds. Sprinkle with salt and pepper. In a bowl, mix the bread crumbs, scallions, basil, garlic, parsley, oregano, and salt. Fill the tomatoes with the bread crumb mixture. Bake for 15 minutes or until lightly browned and tender. Sprinkle with cheese and olive oil and brown in the oven for another minute.

> "It's difficult to think anything but pleasant thoughts while eating a homegrown tomato."
>
> —Lewis Grizzard

Baked Beans

Baked beans: An American staple for centuries. Whether you're prepping for a camping trip or enjoying the dog days of summer at a barbecue, now you can prepare this classic without the preservatives and artificial ingredients from the can.

Yield: 4–6 servings

4 cups dried navy beans, soaked overnight

1 medium onion, peeled and halved

4 whole cloves

8 ounces bacon or salt pork, cubed

¼ cup maple syrup

¼ cup dark molasses

2 teaspoons mustard powder

2 tablespoons dark rum

Pinch of salt and freshly ground black pepper

Combine ingredients in a 4-quart slow cooker. Turn on low and cook for 6 to 8 hours.

Vegetable Gratin

Add a bit of crunch to this hearty veggie dish with a beautifully browned layer of seasoned panko crust. The warming scents of nutmeg and garlic will fill your kitchen, making your guests feel right at home.

Yield: 2-4 servings

2 tablespoons butter

2 medium zucchini, sliced crosswise

2 medium yellow squash, sliced crosswise

2 shallots, minced

2 garlic cloves, minced

Pinch of salt and freshly ground black pepper

½ cup heavy cream

¼ teaspoon nutmeg

1 cup panko crumbs

½ cup Parmesan cheese, grated

Preheat oven to 450°F. Melt butter over medium heat in a large skillet. Add zucchini, yellow squash, shallots, and garlic. Season with salt and pepper. Cook, stirring occasionally, for 4 minutes or until vegetables are crisp, but not thoroughly cooked. Stir in cream and nutmeg for 3 to 5 minutes or until thickened. Remove from heat and stir in ½ cup panko crumbs, ½ cup Parmesan, and a sprinkle of salt and pepper. Pour into a baking dish and add the remaining panko crumbs over the surface. Bake for 8 to 10 minutes or until the top is golden brown.

Popovers

Popovers are the savory American twist on the Yorkshire Pudding of England. It's a light fluffy roll, served sweet topped with whipped cream for a breakfast treat or with afternoon tea, or with meats for lunch or dinner. This easy recipe calls for a popover pan, but a muffin tin works perfectly, too!

Yield: 12 popovers

4 tablespoons (½ stick) unsalted butter, melted

6 eggs, lightly beaten

2 cups milk

2 cups all-purpose flour

1 teaspoon salt

Preheat an oven to 450°F. Grease the cups of a popover pan with butter or nonstick spray. Pour ½ teaspoon of melted butter into each well. Whisk the eggs and milk, followed by 2 tablespoons of melted butter. In a separate bowl, mix the flour and salt. Add in the egg mixture, stirring until smooth. Pour the batter into the popover wells and bake for 20 minutes. Reduce the heat to 325°F and cook for another 15 minutes. To remove popovers from pan, invert over a cooling rack. Repeat the cooking process for the remaining popover batter.

"All sorrows are less with bread. "

—Miguel de Cervantes, *Don Quixote*

Zucchini Casserole

Simple only in preparation but not in flavor, this zucchini casserole is more than the sum of its parts. Ripe with an array of fantastic fresh vegetables, fragrant herbs, and melted cheese, this piping hot casserole should make its way onto your table time and time again.

Yield: 6–8 servings

4 tablespoons butter

1 yellow onion, diced

2 cloves garlic, minced

1 large zucchini, sliced

1 large summer squash

1 cup sliced mushrooms

1 cup sweet corn

1 tablespoon dried basil

1 teaspoon dried oregano

½ teaspoon salt

12 ounces shredded cheese, such as mozzarella or Fontina

3 eggs, beaten

Chives, chopped, for garnish

Preheat the oven to 375°F. Heat the butter in a large sauté pan over medium high. Stir in the onion, garlic, zucchini, squash, and mushrooms. Stir for a minute and then add the corn, sautéing for 5 to 7 minutes or until tender but not overcooked. Remove from the heat and mix in the basil, oregano, and salt. Add cheese and eggs and pour the mixture into a greased casserole dish or pie pan. Add extra zucchini slices on top and sprinkle with more cheese. Bake for 20 minutes, covered with foil. Remove foil and bake for another 5 to 10 minutes to brown. Sprinkle with chives before serving.

Polenta Pizza

Spice up your pizza night with this fun take on the old standard. Instead of traditional pizza crust, the delicious toppings lie on a bed of polenta that provides incredible texture. Perfect when sharing a plate with a fresh green salad or roasted vegetables, this is an all-new way to enjoy a mealtime favorite.

Yield: 4 servings

2½ cups chicken broth

2 cloves garlic, minced

1 cup polenta or yellow stone-ground cornmeal

Pinch of salt and freshly ground black pepper

¼ cup grated Parmesan

1½ tablespoons olive oil

¼ cup sun-dried tomatoes, thinly sliced

4 ounces mozzarella, sliced

½ cup cherry tomatoes, sliced in half

½ teaspoon dried oregano

½ teaspoon dried basil

Heat oven to 425°F. In a large saucepan, bring chicken broth and garlic to a boil over medium-high. Reduce the heat to medium-low and slowly add the cornmeal. Stir continuously with a whisk to break down clumps. Add salt and pepper and keep stirring for 4 to 6 minutes or until it thickens. Remove from heat and stir in Parmesan. Brush olive oil onto a 9-inch pan or baking sheet and spread out polenta. Top pizza with sun-dried tomatoes and mozzarella. Finish with cherry tomatoes, oregano, and basil. Bake for 20 to 25 minutes or until polenta crust is crisp.

Vegetable-Stuffed Mushrooms

Stuffed mushrooms have always been a crowd favorite, but most people tend to save them for annual parties or family gatherings. These stuffed mushrooms are too delicious to wait for an event to bring them to the table, so serve them up with a juicy steak or roasted chicken.

Yield: 8–12 servings

24 large white mushrooms

2 tablespoons olive oil

½ medium onion, chopped

3 green onions, chopped

1 red bell pepper

¼ cup roasted red pepper, chopped

1 teaspoon oregano, chopped

¼ cup fresh basil, finely chopped

2 cloves garlic, minced

Pinch of salt and freshly ground black pepper

6 tablespoons bread crumbs

4 tablespoons Parmesan, grated

¼ cup fresh parsley, chopped

Remove and retain stems and allow mushrooms to dry for a few hours or overnight. Preheat oven to 400°F. Heat the olive oil in a skillet over medium heat. Add stems, medium and green onions, and bell and roasted peppers to the skillet. Stir in oregano, basil, garlic, salt, and pepper, sautéing for 5 minutes or until peppers are tender. Transfer to a bowl and blend with bread crumbs, Parmesan, and parsley. Arrange mushrooms cavity-side up on a parchment- or foil-lined baking sheet. Fill cavities with stuffing. Bake for 15 minutes and serve hot.

Cheesy Cauliflower

A casserole like no other, this dish is comforting, cheesy, and delicious. Enhanced by the fresh flavor and great texture of cauliflower, you will want to have it on your table again and again.

Yield: 4–6 servings

1 head cauliflower

1 summer squash, peeled

2 tablespoons butter

½ yellow onion, diced

1 clove garlic, minced

2 tablespoons flour

1½ cups milk

1½ cups sharp Cheddar, shredded

½ cup Parmesan, grated

Pinch of salt and freshly ground black pepper

Preheat oven to 400°F. Break cauliflower into florets and chop squash into cubes. In a large pot, bring water to a boil over high heat. Cook cauliflower for 5 minutes. Strain cauliflower and place into a greased baking dish with squash. Melt butter and heat onion and garlic on medium heat for about 2 minutes or until aromatic and onions are translucent. Whisk in flour for 1 minute, and then slowly add in milk until evenly blended. Stir in and melt cheese, seasoning with salt and pepper. Pour cheese mixture over cauliflower and squash. Bake for 20 to 25 minutes or until cheese is bubbling and tops of cauliflower are browned.

> "The only time to eat diet food is while you're waiting for the steak to cook."
> —Julia Child

Rosemary Crispy Onions

Crunchy onion rings are an old favorite, but this recipe has a hint of something special. With a little bit of rosemary, these onion rings transform from an ordinary burger side to a delectable new favorite.

Yield: 4 servings

1 Vidalia onion, sliced crosswise into rings

2 cups buttermilk

4 cups olive oil

2 cups all-purpose flour, divided in half

2 tablespoons garlic salt

1 tablespoon fresh rosemary, finely chopped

1 tablespoon freshly ground black pepper

12 ounces lager-style beer

Soak onions in buttermilk for 30 minutes to an hour. Heat olive oil in medium saucepan to 375°F. Mix 1 cup flour, garlic salt, rosemary, and pepper in a bowl. Mix 1 cup flour and beer in a separate bowl. Dredge onions in the flour mixture and then the beer batter. Fry for 2 minutes in batches or until golden brown. Remove onions from the oil and set on a cooling rack or plate lined with paper towels to soak up excess oil.

Broccoli Quiche

Not just a breakfast food, this broccoli quiche is a hearty complement to a wide variety of meals. Serve it alongside roasted vegetables or green salad for a wholesome, satisfying feast.

Yield: 8 servings

1 tablespoon unsalted butter

2 cups medium yellow onion, diced

6 large eggs

¾ cup heavy cream

¾ pound broccoli florets, steamed

1 cup sharp Cheddar, grated

Pinch of salt and freshly ground black pepper

Preheat oven to 375°F. Melt the butter in a skillet over medium heat. Add the onion and heat for about 5 to 7 minutes, or until golden. Whisk eggs and cream together in a large bowl. Add onion, broccoli, cheese, salt, and pepper to combine. Pour mixture into an oven-safe dish and cook for 40 to 45 minutes or until cooked through.

"I don't think any day is worth living without thinking about what you're going to eat next at all times."

—Nora Ephron

Galette
Ratatouille

This savory treat pairs summer vegetables with a flaky, buttery crust of fresh pastry. Made up of the vibrant colors of fresh zucchini, squash, and tomatoes, it tastes just as good as it looks.

Yield: 4-8 servings

1½ cups all-purpose flour

¼ teaspoon salt

1 teaspoon dried, ground rosemary

8 tablespoons unsalted butter, cut into small cubes and chilled

¼ cup plain yogurt

2 teaspoons fresh lemon juice

¼ cup ice water

1 zucchini, sliced thinly

1 summer squash, sliced thinly

1 heirloom tomato, sliced thinly

½ cup ricotta cheese

¼ cup Parmesan, grated

¼ teaspoon onion powder

3 garlic cloves, crushed

1 tablespoon olive oil

1 egg yolk, beaten with 1 tablespoon water for egg wash

Combine flour, salt, and rosemary. Mix with butter until well blended. Add the yogurt, lemon juice, and ice water and blend until a ball of dough is formed. Wrap dough and refrigerate for at least one hour. Preheat the oven to 400°F. Prepare vegetables and place in a strainer with salt to drain off excess

water. Pat dry with clean towel before using. Mix the cheeses, onion powder, garlic, and olive oil. Roll out the dough and place on a lined baking sheet that has been sprinkled lightly with flour or cornmeal. Spread the cheese mixture over the dough, leaving about 2 inches of space at the edges. Working from the center, arrange the vegetables in a clockwise spiral until they reach the edge of the cheese. Fold over excess dough to create a crust. Brush the crust with egg wash. Bake in the oven for 40 minutes or until the crust is lightly browned.

Index

A
Acorn Squash, Cranberry-Walnut, 89
almonds, in Wheat Berry & Spinach Salad, 24
Arborio rice. *See* risotto
Artichoke, Roasted, 38
Arugula and Beet Salad, 14
asparagus
   Lemony Asparagus, 42
   Sautéed Asparagus & Quinoa, 71

B
bacon
   in Baked Beans, 106
   Chickpeas with Spinach & Bacon, 54
Baked Beans, 106
Baked Veggie Fries, 53
Balsamic Brussels Sprouts, 41
basil
   in Caprese Salad, 17
   in Vegetable Orzo Pasta Salad, 18
Beans, Baked, 106
beets
   in Baked Veggie Fries, 53
   Beet and Arugula Salad, 14
bell peppers
   in Ratatouille, 57
   Roasted Eggplant and Pepper Mélange, 33
bok choy
   Bok Choy, 50
   Crunchy Bok Choy Salad, 21
   in Pork Fried Rice, 67
broccoli
   Broccoli Quiche, 123
   in Roasted Vegetable Medley, 37
   Sun-Dried Tomato Broccoli, 49
   in Vegetable Orzo Pasta Salad, 18
Broccoli Rabe, Pine Nut, 45
Brussels Sprouts, Balsamic, 41

C
cabbage, in Kohlrabi Slaw, 13
Caprese Salad, 17
carrots
   in Baked Veggie Fries, 53
   in Kohlrabi Slaw, 13
   in Roasted Vegetable Medley, 37
   Walnut Carrots, 61
cauliflower
   Cheesy Cauliflower, 119
   in Roasted Vegetable Medley, 37
Cheese Risotto, Three, 75
Cheese Soufflé, 103
Cheesy Cauliflower, 119
Chickpeas with Spinach & Bacon, 54
Colby Jack Macaroni and Cheese, 77
corn
   Grilled Mexican Corn, 46
   in Zucchini Casserole, 113

Cous Cous Salad, 22
cranberries, dried
   in Cous Cous Salad, 22
   in Wheat Berry & Spinach Salad, 24
Cranberry-Walnut Acorn Squash, 89
Creamed Spinach, 30
Crispy Potato Pancakes, 87
Crunchy Bok Choy Salad, 21

E
eggplant
   in Ratatouille, 57
   Roasted Eggplant and Pepper Mélange, 33
eggs
   in Broccoli Quiche, 123
   in Cheese Soufflé, 103
   in Popovers, 110
   in Tortilla Española, 98

F
feta cheese, in Vegetable Orzo Pasta Salad, 18
Fried Rice, Pork, 67
fries
   Baked Veggie Fries, 53
   Spicy Jicama Fries, 93

G
Galette Ratatouille, 124
Garlicky Green Beans, 29
goat cheese, in Beet and Arugula Salad, 14
gratins
   Potato Gratin, 97
   Vegetable Gratin, 109
Green Beans, Garlicky, 29
Grilled Mexican Corn, 46
Gruyère cheese
   in Cheese Soufflé, 103
   in Tomatoes Provencal, 105

H
Horseradish Mashed Potatoes, 90

J
Jicama Fries, Spicy, 93

K
Kohlrabi Slaw, 13

L
Lemon-Pistachio Swiss Chard, 34
Lemony Asparagus, 42

M
Macaroni and Cheese, Colby Jack, 77
Mashed Potatoes, Horseradish, 90
Mexican Corn, Grilled, 46
mint, in Cous Cous Salad, 22

mozzarella
  in Caprese Salad, 17
  in Polenta Pizza, 115
mushrooms
  in Creamed Spinach, 30
  Mushroom Risotto, 65
  Parmesan Polenta with Sautéed Mushrooms, 80
  Vegetable-Stuffed Mushrooms, 117
  in Zucchini Casserole, 113

O

Onions, Rosemary Crispy, 120
oranges, in Crunchy Bok Choy Salad, 21
Orecchiette with Peas, 73
Orzo Pasta Salad, Vegetable, 18

P

Parmesan Polenta with Sautéed Mushrooms, 80
parsnips, in Baked Veggie Fries, 53
pasta
  Colby Jack Macaroni and Cheese, 77
  Orecchiette with Peas, 73
  Vegetable Orzo Pasta Salad, 18
peas
  Orecchiette with Peas, 73
  in Pork Fried Rice, 67
pine nuts
  Pine Nut Broccoli Rabe, 45
  in Vegetable Orzo Pasta Salad, 18
  in Wheat Berry & Spinach Salad, 24
Pistachio-Lemon Swiss Chard, 34
Pizza, Polenta, 115
polenta
  Parmesan Polenta with Sautéed Mushrooms, 80
  Polenta Pizza, 115
pomegranate, in Cous Cous Salad, 22
Popovers, 110
Pork Fried Rice, 67
potatoes
  Crispy Potato Pancakes, 87
  Horseradish Mashed Potatoes, 90
  Potato Gratin, 97
  Tortilla Española, 98
prosciutto, in Orecchiette with Peas, 73
Pumpkin Quinoa, 79

Q

Quiche, Broccoli, 123
quinoa
  Pumpkin Quinoa, 79
  Sautéed Asparagus & Quinoa, 71
  in Wheat Berry & Spinach Salad, 24

R

ramen noodles, in Crunchy Bok Choy Salad, 21
Rapini (Broccoli Rabe), Pine Nut, 45

Ratatouille, 57
  Galette, 124
Rice, Pork Fried, 67
risotto
  Mushroom Risotto, 65
  Three Cheese Risotto, 75
Roasted Artichoke, 38
Roasted Eggplant and Pepper Mélange, 33
Roasted Vegetable Medley, 37
Rosemary Crispy Onions, 120

S

Sautéed Asparagus & Quinoa, 71
Slaw, Kohlrabi, 13
Soufflé, Cheese, 103
Spicy Jicama Fries, 93
spinach
  Chickpeas with Spinach & Bacon, 54
  Creamed Spinach, 30
  Wheat Berry & Spinach Salad, 24
Sun-Dried Tomato Broccoli, 49
Sweet Potatoes, Thyme, 94
Swiss Chard, Lemon-Pistachio, 34

T

Three Cheese Risotto, 75
Thyme Sweet Potatoes, 94
tomatoes
  in Caprese Salad, 17
  in Galette Ratatouille, 124
  in Ratatouille, 57
  Tomatoes Provencal, 105
  in Vegetable Orzo Pasta Salad, 18
tomatoes, sun-dried
  in Polenta Pizza, 115
  Sun-Dried Tomato Broccoli, 49
Tortilla Española, 98

V

Vegetable Gratin, 109
Vegetable Orzo Pasta Salad, 18
Vegetable-Stuffed Mushrooms, 117

W

walnuts
  in Beet and Arugula Salad, 14
  Cranberry-Walnut Acorn Squash, 89
  Walnut Carrots, 61
Wheat Berry & Spinach Salad, 24

Y

yellow squash, in Vegetable Gratin, 109

Z

zucchini
  in Crunchy Bok Choy Salad, 21
  in Galette Ratatouille, 124
  in Ratatouille, 57
  in Vegetable Gratin, 109
  Zucchini Casserole, 113